THORNS IN THE ROSE

POEMS ABOUT
LOVING, FAILING, RAGING, LEARNING, AND TRYING AGAIN

THORNS IN THE ROSE

POEMS ABOUT
LOVING, FAILING, RAGING, LEARNING, AND TRYING AGAIN

REBECCA TORRELLAS

Thorns in the Rose: First Edition
Copyright © 2025 Rebecca Torrellas.

www.rebeccat.com

All rights reserved.
RawRiot Publishing
Cover by: Book Designs by Shae
Formatting by: Shae Coon
ISBN: 979-8-9990728-1-8

All rights to the work within are reserved for the author and publisher. No part of this publication may be reproduced, stored in a retrieval system, or transmitted in any form or by any means, electronic, mechanical, photocopying, recording, scanning, or otherwise, except as permitted under Section 107 or 108 of the 1976 International Copyright Act, without prior written permission except in brief quotations embodied in critical articles and reviews. All characters, organizations, and events portrayed in this book are either the product of the author's imagination or are used fictitiously.

Audiobook narrated by Cesalina Davidson, Laura Coccimiglio, Amira Judeh, Sarah-Beth Diller, Christie Guidry, Bailey Hampton, and Rachel Brownhill. Audiobook produced by RoseFae Entertainment and Friend Indeed Productions.

Summary: "A collection of poems written between 1995 and 2025 that helped keep my sanity during some of the worst times of my life."

I DEDICATE THIS BOOK:

To Braxton and Brian, I would not be able to do any of this without your support, kisses, hugs, and SO MUCH LOVE! I'm the luckiest and happiest woman in the universe because of you.

To my parents, I'd be absolutely nothing without you, and you've supported me through every up and down I've put you through. Love you!

To Brian's family for embracing us and always being there! Love you!

To my family for always supporting me in every little crazy thing I do, even though you are all so far away from me. Los quiero mucho!

To my friends who have experienced my craziness and are still on this journey with me. Thank you!

To Cesalina Davidson, Laura Coccimiglio, Amira Judeh, Sarah-Beth Diller, Christie Guidry, Bailey Hampton, and Rachel Brownhill, thank you for giving my poetry a voice in the audiobooks and for supporting what I do with your talents and friendships.

To God, because You came up with the original tapestry of my life and knew how to steer it, who to put in it, and who to remove to get the perfect combination I have today — a journey this book celebrates. THANK YOU!!!!!!

Letter From the Author

Dear Reader,

First, thank you for being here! I consider it a privilege that you are taking the time to read my poetry. This is truly a celebration of 30 years of writing. Writing has always been my go-to to relieve any anxiety, pain, rage, stress, happiness, delirium, or sadness I may be experiencing. Sometimes, paper and pen were the confessional I could go to where I knew I wouldn't be judged by whatever feelings I had to express.

I never thought of sharing these works until I cleaned out my attic recently and found a folder of unrecorded songs, unfinished ideas, random scribblings, and tons of poems from anger and pain I've long since moved on from. Some situations almost killed me, and others have been peacefully solved since then. But the one thing that stuck with me as I sat and read all of this was that, at the time, I felt like I was at rock bottom and that nothing would ever work out for me.

When I read the poems I'd written more recently, I realized how far I'd come, how much I'd learned, and how much I'd changed for the better. I made mistakes along the way — A LOT OF THEM — but through all the heartbreaks, the mistakes, the regrets, the rage, and the endless hopelessness, I ended up in the best place in the world. Had I given up at any point, I would've missed the peace and love I have today. I credit my writing these poems as a way to get out all of my emotions, clouding all my senses, to be able to look back, take responsibility for my part, recognize the mistakes others made, and learn from it all, becoming a wiser version of myself.

So, I decided to compile this poetry book full of years of my secret feelings. For better or worse, immature or wise, right or wrong, joy and heartbreak, rage and peace, every emotion I went through is typed in these pages. May they bring you comfort and hope that things do get better and that happiness is within reach, even when you don't see it at the time. Don't give up. Never give up. You'll never know what is around the corner, and it may be all you've ever wanted — thorns and all.

Rebecca Torrellas

The thing about roses is that,
Even if the petals break off and die,
With strong roots and stems,
They can withstand any winter.
If you cut them, they get stronger
And bloom again, thorns and all.
It is in their endurance and resilience
That their true beauty can be
Witnessed in all its splendor.

CONTENTS

Better Off 1
The X 2
The One 4
What's The Point? 6
Mean Girl 8
Show Me 10
You Won't 12
Walk Away 15
My Worst Enemy 17
Better Off 19
Stop Pretending 21
   The Evil 23
Not Your Pretty Girl 24
Un-Me 26
Nothing 29
I Felt Nothing 33
She Left You 35
Mostly You 39
Your Nightmare 44
The Evil 50
   Done 55
Sorry 56
The Knife 60
Karma 62
Done 66
   Half Of My Heart 69
As Long as I'm With You 70

Long Enough	72
We Were Crazy	74
Sweet Temptation	76
I Had Hoped	78
Half Of My Heart	80
Off-Script	82
Arguing With Stars	85
Couldn't Do It	87
Exorcized	89
Changed The Prophecy	92
The So-Called Truth	95
The Exchange	97
I Hope You're Happy	99
If We Saw Each Other Now	101
Witch Hunt	103
Weapons Of Silence	104
Hateful Butterfly	106
Witch Hunt	109
Bodies You Scar	112
You Can Have Her	114
Closure	116
Restoration	119
Scraps	120
The Wreckage	122
Restoration	124
Coffee Vibes	126
Showing Up	128
Ready To Be Home	130
At Last	131

I Remember It All 133
Headline 134
Holding On to Nothing 137
Disrespected 139
I Remember It All 141
Will I? 143
Stupid One 144
Stage Fright 146
Change Your Mind 148
End Of the Tunnel 151
Winning Streak 152
The End of The Tunnel 157

WELCOME

Welcome to my life.
Come and read my story
An opportunity to claim
My impending victory.

I stayed quiet for years and years
Letting karma be the key.
Observing all their fallouts
That happened without me.

I wrote and wrote
But kept it locked.
All this time thinking
All of it was my fault.

So now I take a moment
To give my point of view.
The words I'm afraid to say,
But, when I write, they're true.

The madness that preceded
The peace I feel today.
The blessings that appeared
After I cried my life away.

I hope the words I've typed
Help others to hold on.
You never know the beauty
That may suddenly come along.

So, I present to you
The words I never said.
Finding closure
By revisiting the dead.

These are the thorns
The rose bloomed to exile.
My side of the journey.
I hope you'll stay a while.

REBECCA TORRELLAS

BETTER OFF

REBECCA TORRELLAS

THE X

While you wasted time just thinking of yourself
I took care of the man I wanted for myself.
I gave all of my heart; a chance I had to take.
Wiping my tears, waiting for your mistake.

I'm sorry, girl. That's just way too bad.
You took for granted the love you had.
Take your heart and move on to the next.
It's too late now; you're the X.

You wanted him to give up so much for you.
He asked for a compromise, but you refused to.
Now you're calling, trying to get him back.
My unconditional love is stronger than your attack.

I was there when you broke his heart.
To put together the world you tore apart.
I made him smile when you made him cry.
Did everything you refused to try.

Don't pick a fight. There's no reason to.
The only one who messed up was you.
I won his heart, and now I'm next.
I'm his love; you're the X.

THE ONE

I've fallen in love again
Stronger than the time before.
For a while, I didn't think
Love existed anymore.

I want to be with you, but
I'm also scared of you.
Scars of the past make
Me fear something new.

I want to be the one you adore;
To be the girl of your desire;
Who is everything you need.
I want to be the one.

When you sleep at night
Do you dream about me?
And when you wake up
Is it me you want to see?

I know how you feel, but I can't
Help the insecurity.
Your indecision
Is slowly killing me.

Is it yes, or is it no?
If you love me, tell me so.
Is the check on "yes" or "no"?
I would really like to know.

WHAT'S THE POINT?

He tells me I'm beautiful.
Something I've heard before.
He tells me so many things
Yet never wants more.

                      What is it he wants from me?
                          He doesn't even know.
                       There's so much love in me
                            That I can't even show.

So what's the point
To call me beautiful?
It doesn't do much for me
If the heart isn't full.

                        Some have said I'm beautiful
                          Then turn the other way
                            To someone they don't
                              Love enough, anyway.

REBECCA TORRELLAS

If I'm really that beautiful,
Then what's missing in me?
Why even bother with the motions
If it's not meant to be?

                    I want to believe in love,
                    But it doesn't want to stay.
                    When something comes around
                    It goes someone else's way.

"How long has it been
Since I called you beautiful?"
That's all he says to me,
So much it's almost pitiful.

                    I ask you if you love me,
                    I never get a reply.
                    You just call me beautiful.
                    I wish I could say goodbye.

MEAN GIRL

I'm behind the chair with my whip in hand
Trying to tame the beast within you
That roams away from my cage of love.
The one I want to force you into.

I'm a mean girl trained to attack,
Making plans to hold you back.
I'm the hunter; you are the prey.
This time, I will have my way.

As you run from your illness of love,
I'm stuck playing part-time lover.
I wish I had the strength to walk away,
But I'm afraid that you'll recover.

I'm a mean girl chasing you down.
Ready to wear my crown.
I'm a princess, too good to play.
You're here to stay or go away.

REBECCA TORRELLAS

I'm not asking you to marry me
Or to buy me a diamond ring.
But the blanks are confusing me,
And I'm tired of wondering.

I'm a mean girl who wants to be loved.
So tired of being pushed and shoved.
Will you keep me or throw me away?
You can't decide, so I guess I'll stay.

Show Me

Don't just tell me you care.
Don't just say you love me.
I don't want to just hear it.
I don't want to imagine it.

Show me your love.
Act like you care.
I want to experience it.
I want to remember it.

That way, when I talk about you
It won't be about what you say.
It'll be about who you are
And how it feels to be loved by you.

But if you're ashamed of who I am,
If you can't love me like I want,
Then save me the effort
And walk away.

I'm worth being loved.
I'm worth feeling cherished.
The ending will hurt,
But someone else will love me better.

YOU WON'T

Life should be
Lived without limits.
You're the one
Who tries everything once,
Never afraid of anything.
Why are you
Afraid of me?

Have you not yet
Felt completed?
Has your fulfillment
Been my flaw?
I try to punctuate
Your sentences,
But they still
Don't come out right.

Turn all the lights out,
But you won't.
Bring on the moonlight,
But you don't.

Is this a life
You don't want to know?
Show me your fire,
You won't.

In your room
You sit in peace,
While I'm attempting
To break down walls.
I'm running empty
On the patience fuel
As you overlook
The gauge.

And you know
I'm waiting.
And you know
I'm willing.
What good does
It do me
When you don't
Know what you want?

And I've been
Good to you.
Unconditional

To a fault.
So, end it,
Or seal it.
There's no
Other way now.

I should walk away
But I can't.
Because I know
The door just
Means goodbye.
Would you follow me?
I already know…

You won't.

I am broken, shattered, and thrown away.
I've been beaten down by kind words.
Don't say any more; you're killing me slowly.
Have the heart to walk away.

Fine, just stay. It won't help anyway.
Nothing you say will soften the pain.
All your words just turn the knife.
It's more humane if you walk away.

Who are you to tell me how I should feel?
Who made you the expert on the two of us?
I don't want to hear it. What is it going to change?
Just turn around and walk away.

Being friends won't heal the wound.
There's no band-aid for you leaving me.
Your guilt can't heal my broken heart.
I'd feel better if you would walk away.

You're still here when there's nothing to save.
You never loved me anyway.
Enough. I wish you the best in life.
Please close the door as you walk away.

MY WORST ENEMY

Was I the last to know
That we are at the end?
Was I the only one
With silly dreams in her head?

It seemed you wanted me.
When did it fade?
You must've been faking to me
Or just playing pretend.

Where did we go wrong?
I was too blind to see.
How did it all go down
For you being with me?

Who do you think you are
Giving me away?
You're tearing me apart
And running away.

I guess there are no explanations
That will change this now.
I won't wish time to go back.
It won't end with a vow.

I should've known from the start
I was a placeholder for another girl.
You were meant to break my heart
And blow up my whole world.

Denial is no longer my friend.
It's too clear to see.
You were my best friend
Now, my worst enemy.

BETTER OFF

I gave you moons,
I gave you planets.
I offered more than I could give.
I knew returns were limited,
But I was hoping to gain your respect.

>I tried to be what you wanted.
>But my best wasn't good enough.
>My passion for pleasing
>Went far beyond normal means
>And led me to the exit door.

You took me in,
Then you threw me out.
Made it sound like a good thing.
Maybe one day I'll understand why,

But don't expect a thank you card.

> I'm sure I'll get over it
> And open another door.
> After I'm done
> Counting change for bread,
> I won't remember anymore.

My passion was overflowing.
You didn't see it for yourself.
I hope my successor
Can help you make the millions
I plan to make on my own.

> I'm sure you mean well,
> And it's for the best.
> I trust that what you say is true.
> So I'll move on and be a success
> Since I'm better off without you.

STOP PRETENDING

Do you think I don't know the truth?
I know exactly what went behind my back.
So don't play Mr. Innocent,
'Cause you don't know how to act.

You never said, "I love you."
Those words meant nothing in your mind.
But you brainwashed me to need you
So, I wouldn't leave you behind.

I believed in your actions
And the promises you delayed to make.
I trusted you to be faithful;
That was my biggest mistake.

So stop acting, stop pretending
That you loved me, I don't need you.
Go to your other and keep pretending
You'll be faithful to her, too.

REBECCA TORRELLAS

THE EVIL

NOT YOUR PRETTY GIRL

I'm not a gorgeous girl;
The criteria doesn't fit me.
I'm not a little girl;
I make a killing being curvy.

>I'm an original,
>I don't hide behind the lipstick.
>I can't play the girly-girl
>Because I'm a misfit.

I won't dye my hair
So I can look good to you.
I won't change my style
Only because you ask me to.

>I'm not clay to mold,
>So don't play that game.
>I'm not undiscovered ground
>So, don't stake your claim.

REBECCA TORRELLAS

Tell me what you want,
I'll do my best to deliver.
If I don't like your request,
Then you'll have to reconsider.

                              I'm not here to serve,
                            But I will be good to you.
                         I'm not a damsel in distress,
                           There's no need for rescue.

You're not an architect,
So don't attempt to design me.
You can't handle tools,
So don't try to construct me.

                                I am not for sale,
                        So I'll never be your property.
                              I'm not your slave,
                              So don't control me.

Don't attempt to modify me,
If I don't fit into your world.
I'm not lost, so don't come find me.
I'm not your pretty girl.

UN-ME

I'm not one to feel lonely.
Love to dance in the rain.
Just floating through life
Laughing through the pain.

But lately, the fire
Always in my heart
Seems to fade into embers
Has me falling apart.

Can you tell?

I'm second-guessing
Every move I make
Trying to please you, support you
Wait for give and take.

But what am I getting?
I just don't know
My passion is dying
There's barely a glow.

Unpretty, unfun, unloved, unhappy
Everything I never wanted to be.
Unwanted, unjust, unkind, unsexy
I'm tired of feeling so un-me.

I try to give you
All the things you wanted
But it's always changing
Before it even started.

Am I missing something?

I can't keep up.
It's worse than the tide
You're in and you're out
I run, and I hide.

I don't recognize me at all.
Covered in dust you leave behind.
I got a total stranger
Dictating how I should live my life.

I know I'm not perfect
My flaws are still part of me.
Look in my eyes
Do you see anything left of me?

Unloved, untrusted, unsmart, unhappy
You're making me think this is all I can be.
Unwanted, unkind, unjust, unsexy
I'm tired of feeling so un-me.

NOTHING

You told me you loved me
And put me on a pedestal
Only to enslave me
The moment I said, "I love you."
I went from a star in your sky
To the dirt you'd stomp around
Making me think I was a nobody
To cater to your everything.

I became a manager
Held cameras
To make you look bigger
Than you were.
I had to eat certain things
And go to sleep by the time you said.
I was in a cage I never noticed
Was in the room.

You made me feel like I was nothing.
Nothing. Nothing. NOTHING.

And nothing I felt was better
Or worse than what you felt.
All my feelings put on a shelf
They weren't even worth mentioning.
You'd get mad if I moved in my sleep
Because it woke you up.
Many nights, you'd sleep on the bed
I bought while I slept on the couch.

I wanted to better myself, you'd say
"What about me?"
Making me feel bad like I
Was destroying our partnership.
But it wasn't a partnership.
It was you commanding and me obeying.
And if I fought for myself, you'd say
The world would be better if I were dead.

You made me feel like I was nothing.
Nothing. Nothing. NOTHING.

And I stayed quiet, blaming myself for everything.
While you told people I was the loser

Then, you told me you loved me on the same day.
You wanted an excuse for not being there
When I needed you the most.
But you were a director
You only mattered.
So, you let me suffer.

You wanted me to die,
So you were happy letting me.
Then came back around
Saying you wanted me back
Bringing a 12-paged contract
I'd have to abide by
To stay by your side.
I left and never looked back.

I had to go back to find something.
I was more than NOTHING.

Fast forward to these days.
You're alone yet again.
I assumed you were happy
Since I never checked on you,
Which was weird.
You would think I'd care
But I didn't. You took it all out of me

Making me believe it was me all these years.

Now look at me with my stories to tell
Making money from the art that I create.
Being teachable, coachable, and bettering myself.
The parts you wouldn't allow me to do.
And it seems your old tricks didn't work again.
The third one ran away; you need a better cage.
Maybe actually learn how to love
Rather than get a girl to play the part you want.

And make them feel like they're something.
Outside of you, we're EVERYTHING!

I FELT NOTHING

I just saw a picture of you.
You look well. You look happy.
I never imagined
That it wouldn't affect me.

I felt nothing.

It was so weird,
I was looking at a stranger.
I promised you forever
And it doesn't even matter?

I felt nothing.

The last thing I ever thought
Was that I could turn so cold.
It's so surprising
I've never told a soul.

I felt nothing.

Where's the part of me
That used to love you?
Am I still capable of loving
If I barely remember you?

I felt nothing.

I hope you stay well,
And that your heart is mended.
The pain I caused you
Was never intended.

But I felt nothing.

SHE LEFT YOU

For years, you called me The Evil, and I wore it
Like a scarlet letter, quietly believing it.
Always saying I was horrible.
Made me so ashamed to be me.

All the roles I played to make you shine.
I tried to help, and you told me I was awful.
How dare I question anything?
You knew everything.

I worked hard, yet isolated and hated.
One drama after another; you, my victim.
I fought hard to try and be your hero.
Yet you only kept a list of my mistakes.

You say you did your best art with me.
Has it occurred to you why?
I left so much blood, sweat, and tears,
And you still won't give me credit for it.

Repeatedly, we'd have the same arguments.
You, the innocent, dealing with all my defects.
Telling my folks you were disappointed in me
And isolating me with lies.

All I did was blame myself for everything.
I ran away, and you love-bombed me back
Only to tell me you hated me with every breath.
And I lost myself more and more each day.

Your first love yelled you were controlling.
You said they were lies; I didn't listen.
You had me convinced she was crazy.
Her truth echoes in hindsight.

In a cage and scrutinized,
I didn't deserve love.
I had to leave however I could,
You deserved better than me anyway.

Then I heard you met someone
Better for you than me.
She seemed sweet and really loved you
And that gave me peace.

REBECCA TORRELLAS

I barely knew who I'd become
Why did I do things I'd never done before?
I needed answers, my therapist yelled,
"Do you realize what you were reacting to?"

I fell in love again, but I wouldn't dare
To let him know who I really was.
You had destroyed every ounce of me and
Made me ashamed I was alive.

Who would want me? I wasn't anything.
I was The Evil... all that was left of me.
And I let that wound grow into a rabbit hole.
Any blessing brought impostor syndrome.

Then she left you, sick of your emotional abuse.
She was braver than I'd ever been.
She knew what you were doing and had enough.
Saw through the gaslighting and victimization I missed.

And suddenly, everything made sense.
Before me and after me the same result.
It wasn't me that lost who she was.
You took everything I loved about myself.

And now I'm free! I remember who I am
And who I was always supposed to be.
I'm loved again, and old friends have come back around.
What was so lost is finally found.

My conscience feels unburdened.
You drove me crazy; I was reacting to it.
But when she left you, I felt vindicated.
My guilt was no longer manipulated.

There you are: wash, rinse, repeat.
I'm here more loved than ever before.
My imperfect house is my loving home.
No one strays; it's honest love.

Feels so good to finally heal.
Keep your abuse going; I don't care.
You won't break my happy place.
You can't control me; that's why you hate me.

MOSTLY YOU

So, here we are
Over a decade gone.
I'm soaring in love
And look at you...

The things I never said
The abuse my mind took
Were silent in my head.
And now you're alone.

So, it was you.
I took the blame,
Bathed in shame,
I was the bad guy.

The cheater, the liar
The lazy, The Evil
I took it and took it
Just to stay sane.

REBECCA TORRELLAS

You made me the enemy
Even to my family.
I was isolated and controlled.
I was running away.

I lost my identity.
The loyalty, the love, the fun.
I looked for me everywhere
Because you drained me.

You made me miserable.
I hated living.
You made me feel worthless,
Fighting for an ounce of dignity.

But when I fought, I was crazy.
When I sat back, I was useless.
When I made art, you wanted the credit.
When I followed, you didn't appreciate it.

But thank karma
For shining the truth.
You're alone again, writhing in pain
While I'm in love and happy.

It was always you.
About you. For you. With you.
To shine, shine, shine above all.
And make me dark and insignificant.

You were left again.
Not at my hand.
Not by my words.
Not by my prayers.

So it was you
Building your misery.
Three times over...
Don't you even get it?

Your exes are all friends
And you're never spoken about.
The lives we have after you
Far surpassing in significance.

You made us your enemy
Loving only for yourself.
And your women's needs
Dispensable at best.

Always the victim, yet
Acting as the hero,
Shaming enemies you should've
Long forgotten about.

But you love misery
Promoting your villains
All who have long moved on
Until you post another rant.

Karma police was on patrol
I never wished for this gift at my door.
Vindication for all to see.
The curtain's open; the spotlight is yours.

So, it was you.
Reality strikes.
Keep finger-pointing,
Never learn your lesson.

The cycle repeats.
Find your next victim.
Maybe number four
Will suit you better.

All the words I kept silent
I never had to say.
You were going to screw it up
Your own way.

You'll never learn,
Narcissist man.
Not even fatherhood
Could teach you about life.

So, it was you,
You, you, you.
Your war is your stage.
Blood is your starlet.

Thank you for letting
Everyone know
That it wasn't all me
It was mostly you.

REBECCA TORRELLAS

YOUR NIGHTMARE

Close your eyes
Listen for a noise
Make sure it's dark
So I can come in
From inside your mind
Where I live rent free
Haunting you endlessly
With evil memories
Of the heartbreak
You hold on to
Because I escaped
Stupid me
When I turned around
Should've left you there
Writhing in the pain
You earned
When you made me
A slave to manifest
Your happiness
And put mine aside
Gaslighting me

That I was the bad guy
For wanting to dream
You made me feel
Worthless as you lied
To my family, trying
To get them to hate me
Lying to my friends
So they'd cancel me
Isolating me so
You could control me
I tried to leave
Like an idiot I came back
The guilt was too strong
I deserved the pain
Too bad for you
I won anyway
I got my house
My job, my art
My love, my son
My friends, my family
Making money
Using the talents
You still try to
Take credit for
Your little nightmare
I truly am

You prayed for my
Death and destruction
How sad
I prayed you'd be happy
You screwed that up
But blame me for it
When I haven't been
Around you for over a decade
"The Evil is lurking"
Bring me a broom
I swept up my victim
That's always been you
Now you cry because
I'm happier than you
You poor little thing
What a pity
I was in silence
Doing my thing
Like a phoenix in winter
I reclaimed my name
History repeated
And unveiled your sins
Time the redeemer
Of ghosts that you
Wrongly accuse
In the endless effort

To make yourself look better
Lessons ignored
Wisdom rejected
Pointing your fingers
Ignoring the mirrors
The petulant child
Lies screaming in bed
"Look what they've done"
Yet no one is listening
So go to bed
And I'll say "Boo"
Make sure you call
Your angels who keep
Facepalming at your failed
Attempts to hide under rugs
The way you treat
The ones you "love"
"I got my possessions"
"My mannequins shall dance"
"And proclaim my name"
"As their lord and savior"
You were charming once
You act a great game
Then in one swoop
You change the rules
"Change your name"

"Sing for me"
"Break your back"
"You owe it to me"
"Do what I tell you"
"Here are the lines"
"Don't change a thing"
"I'm the mastermind"
"Sing this song I wrote"
"About abusing you"
"You deserve everything"
"I do to you"
"Screw your feelings"
"I've got my life"
"I'm not here for you"
"It's your fault"
"You messed up"
"I'm the perfect man"
"You're the useless one"
"Put on a smile"
"I made a movie"
"I'm the star"
"Look beautiful"
"Make me look good"
"Your pain doesn't matter"
"It's all about me"
"It's always about me"

REBECCA TORRELLAS

"Your only worth
Was and is only me"
I got away
I got away
I got away
And that's
What haunts you
To this very day

Boo!

THE EVIL

I'm The Evil, yet I'm the one making money.
I'm The Evil, yet I'm the one in a long-term loving relationship.
I'm The Evil, yet I have all the friends you backstabbed.
I'm The Evil, yet I'm friends with all your exes.
I'm The Evil, yet you still try to make money off me.
I'm The Evil, yet karma bit your back, not mine.
I'm The Evil, even though you're the one that discards friends after they're no longer useful.
I'm The Evil for realizing you wanted to hold me back.
I'm The Evil for keeping the cats you planned to quarantine in a tiny room for life.
I'm The Evil for wanting credit for my work.
I'm The Evil for never saying anything bad about you until this.
I'm The Evil, who was the only one to miss your narcissism until I almost lost my life.
I'm The Evil because I'm making money from my art.
I'm The Evil because your exes are happier without you.
I'm The Evil because I've been faithful to everyone else.

I'm The Evil because you were the only man I ever felt I had to get away from.

I'm The Evil because I refused to take over payments for a house I couldn't afford.

I'm The Evil because decades later, you're still too bitter to function.

I'm The Evil because you treat women as slaves of your art and not as women you care about.

I'm The Evil because you want to be 25 in a 95-year-old body.

I'm The Evil because I have a man who can build and care for a house, not just say he can and never do it.

I'm The Evil because I have a man who loves me and is my partner without having to be his secretary, manager, maid, assistant, editor, camera person, and more for free while also being a punching bag.

I'm The Evil because you still sell films of your first ex-wife even though she asked you not to, but they're your movies, and you think you own her body and don't give her a dime for it.

I'm The Evil because you got "infamous" for all the wrong reasons.

I'm The Evil because I opened my eyes to your selfishness too late to turn around.

I'm The Evil because you wanted to control what I ate, what I said, what I thought, what medicines I took, what time I went to bed, and how many times we'd have sex regardless of how I was feeling.

I'm The Evil because you pretend to be happy on camera and refuse to smile when they're off.

I'm The Evil because you refused to take care of me after my miscarriages.

I'm The Evil because being with you meant giving up my identity.

I'm The Evil because I wanted off your military branch.

I'm The Evil because being with you meant having no life of my own.

I'm The Evil because you wanted to isolate me from friends and family.

I'm The Evil because you'd lie to my parents to get us into fights all the time to make yourself out to be the hero.

I'm The Evil because I burned 12 pages of your rules while family and friends laughed.

I'm The Evil because roses were always my thing, and you know it.

I'm The Evil because you're lying about having sole custody.

I'm The Evil because you're scared of all the truths I never said about you.

I'm The Evil because you're the one that keeps it like a badge of honor.

I'm The Evil because making yourself the victim is your favorite role.
I'm The Evil because you deserve every ounce of my spite.
I'm The Evil because leaving you is the best thing I've ever done for myself.
I'm The Evil because I was blessed with all I ever wanted after being rid of you.
I'm The Evil because I won the breakup, the fallout, and the aftermath.
I'm The Evil, and I embrace the name like a superhero.

REBECCA TORRELLAS

REBECCA TORRELLAS

DONE

REBECCA TORRELLAS

S❂RRY

I did everything to save the friendship,
I'm not sure why I even bothered.
I'd told you I didn't want more.
It challenged you to force it.

And for a time, I let it go.
I pushed it back, trying to forget.
Figured it was just part of it all.
You said you "loved" me, so I excused it.

You claimed, and you roared.
"You're the 'love' of my life," you said.
Too weak to fight for myself,
I turned my cheek instead.

Then you found access to money.
You stabbed my back to get your win.
And I got canceled before anyone knew
You were guilty as sin.

I had lost so much back then.
I saved things I should've thrown away.
Hanging on for dear life to the people
That were killing me every day.

Interesting thing, the passage of time.
Anxiety struck; I went to therapy.
And as if by a snap of magical forces
It triggered that night and flooded my memory.

I was drunk. You were with my roommate.
You snuck into my room so we could talk
About everything you were feeling
And why I wanted it to stop.

You got on top; I pushed you away.
I told you "no" to save our story.
You didn't care; you did it anyway.
And at the end, you said, "Sorry."

Clearly, in my brain now, that word remains.
The dagger that should've been the end.
I finally have to come to terms with the truth
While you go and play pretend.

I don't regret not telling you off.
I got a miracle out of my silence.
I've made my life a beautiful journey
While memories play with your conscience.

Or maybe they don't; I don't care.
I won the war, if only in my head.
Your wife likely still checks on me
Angry that I'm not lonely, unhappy, or dead.

It's no surprise that I'm not the only one.
Found out you tried to force another.
She faked a seizure to get away
And never spoke to you after.

You told us she was the villain
When she stopped coming around. Amazing
what happens years later
When truths that were lost get found.

So, keep making people bleed.
Crying and pretending they're wrong.
Cut the ties. Tell your lies.
"They wronged me" is your favorite song.

But I know better. I know your secrets,
Some I've disguised as fiction for entertainment.
I keep the truth locked; it would make you cry
To expose those demons in your basement.

To the miracle, thank you for that lead.
I took time to heal and grow and got rewarded.
Truth be told, had we still been talking
You and your wife would've tried to thwart it.

In the end, I was always your enemy;
The ending and beginning of our story.
You knew what you were doing when you did it.
You tried to fix it immediately after with "Sorry."

But I won in the end, and you know it.
I know you're no angel, to her insecure dismay.
Secret emails and under-the-table thigh feels;
It's no secret to anyone the games you play.

Rewarded by God's mercy, He saw what you did.
So, keep living your life with the secrets you keep.
This story is no longer mine; I'm at peace.
"Sorry" for sharing. I'm sure you will weep.

THE KNIFE

Oh, look! There's your knife again
In my back where you love to stab it
Over and over to save your skin.
Sit and cry and blame it on me.

Every day, something new comes out;
Another lie you threw about.
I'd live under a bus if it were up to you.
Never fully killing me to take all the blame.

Cry and claim, "It's all her fault."
While I'm not aware of what's going on.
Then no one wants to deal with me
Until they tell me later what you said.

Well, I'm glad the bus has since exploded
And I'm nowhere near you to blame
Freedom is mine on this side of the bridge
Burned to ashes with bombs of lies.

REBECCA TORRELLAS

I hope your secrets one day rise
And no one is there to hear your cries.
It's what you deserve, and you know it.
Your self-indulgence will be your demise.

You want me dead? That's too bad.
I'm better without your knife in my back.
Others will buy your excuses and tears
And tell me later what a weakling you are.

So much money you took, and you burned.
Trust in you and your incomparable talent.
Burn it on awards to fill your ego.
Then close it all up so no one gets money.

Like a bureau for complaints, the stories
arrive. All the souls you burned in your wake
Hating they ever believed in you
As you run and hide, blaming everyone else.

I'm glad I learned my lesson and left.
And in my smoke, the reveal — you're a joke.
One day, I'll reveal the secrets I've kept.
They won't go with me to my grave, I promise.

KARMA

Does it hurt to see me
Have everything I wanted?
Does it make your ego bleed?

It's gotta sting a little bit.
You accidentally led me to it.
Thank you for the lead.

I bet your wife is seething
That karma awarded me
After all the burns you both inflicted.

I'm glad you didn't know
A baby was coming into my life.
You would've stopped it; I'm sure.

Since your wife wants me dead.
You would've stabbed my back again,
And ruined me to make her proud.

Believe me, it's all gotten back to me.
All the hate she has toward me
And that I'm not in a grave.

That's how it's been for years.
I hid so much out of fear.
Glad karma dried up my tears.

I'll never see either of you again.
Got the best part out of it.
I was rewarded for letting you go.

It feels good to get it out of me.
Not much happiness in our history.
Denial was my friend.

Bridges burned have mended
Except for the two of you.
And that's how it will stay.

I'm living much better
Without the gas lighter
Blowing up my life.

Asking me for help while
Telling others how horrible I am.
Karma came back around.

REBECCA TORRELLAS

I'm finding success on my own
Not screwing investors out of cash.
I learned not to be like you.

I hope you keep burning bridges.
Screwing up and hiding
Is all you know how to do.

I'm not pulling punches anymore.
I've heard everything you've said and more.
I now rejoice I'm dead to you.

Because in my "death"
I'm now safe from
All the destruction you cause.

After karma rewarded me.
I'm seeing everything more clearly.
Not going back for anything.

I've got everything I need.
How life has blessed me.
Don't want to lose a thing.

You'll probably read this
And for once, you won't cry
Cause you never cared.

But karma did...

DONE

I'm done being angry with you;
An anger I've quietly possessed.
I'm done trying to keep quiet
The memories I repressed.

I've screamed to the sky
And cursed your name to clouds.
The wind relieving me of burden
And taking away all my doubts.

No matter how I spin it,
I have him because of you.
The path laid out before me
Came clearly into view.

Now, he's here
And your job is done.
I have found no greater love
Than the life of my son.

REBECCA TORRELLAS

So, we are now strangers
And that is just fine.
I'm living my best life
With this world only mine.

I'm not sure how you are
Or how your life may end.
But thank you for this life,
When you were never my friend.

REBECCA TORRELLAS

REBECCA TORRELLAS

HALF OF MY HEART

REBECCA TORRELLAS

As Long As I'm With You

My heart is racing.
I'm seeing you again for the first time.
After all that we've been through,
You're mine.

Let's runaway.
There's a path laid out just waiting.
It won't be easy,
But we'll be fine.

As long as I'm with you.
Wherever the road leads.
From here to destiny,
My passion is you.

Kiss me again.
I'm addicted to how you touch me.
You can make my heart melt
With just your eyes.

Dreaming away.
We have nothing to lose.
Let's rewrite the soundtrack
Of our lives.

Whatever it takes
I know there's no failure in sight.
Just wish on a shooting star
And we'll be alright.

As long as I'm with you.
Fate, do as you will.
Here to eternity
Always with you.

LONG ENOUGH

Can't seem to find the words
To describe how I feel.
You've brought new breath to my life
Too precious to conceal.

This love that fills my soul
Is dying to come out.
This taste in my mouth
I don't want to live without.

I prayed so much for you to come
After other loves went wrong.
With new meaning to life
Forever's not that long.

With the smile on your face
I've conquered the world.
I miscalculated just how much
This love was worth.

REBECCA TORRELLAS

I've had a beautiful life
I want to share it with you.
Without you by my side
Life seems such a lonely view.

If I had you the rest of my life
It wouldn't be long enough.
Together after we pass
Just might get close enough.

I know it's complicated,
And forever can be tough.
With all I've had in my life,
Your love is more than enough.

REBECCA TORRELLAS

WE WERE CRAZY

I wasn't heroin
And I wasn't a heroine.
Still, you were addicted
To loving me.

You preached about truths
And held your holy Bible.
Then lied to meet me
Anywhere I summoned.

We were crazy.
Driving hours to meet
At 1 a.m. in towns where
Everyone was sleeping.

Yet they saw us as
Star crossed lovers
Chemistry exploding
With every breath.

A connection so vivid
It lit up all the rooms
We went into.
We couldn't hide it.

Our atmosphere
Charged up the planet
We both felt the surge
When our eyes connected.

The ecstasy and agony
Both led to the same end.
Entangled truths and lies
Creating our orbit.

Maybe we should be grateful
We all survived it.
Intoxicating, maddening
How did we do it?

Maybe one day we'll
Leave our asylums
And taste it again.
Until then ...

SWEET TEMPTATION

Are we a curse or a miracle?
You got me addicted; I can't let go.
I'd die for this; it's out of control.
All the chemicals explode.

Am I a goddess or a slut
Risking my righteousness
For the sweet temptation
Of a stud or the devil himself?

Our secret language;
You know how to melt me.
I can't think; I feel so dumb
Ecstasy beyond dreaming.

You're digging deep in my heart
Covering all the bullet holes
Shot by previous villains
Who messed with my head.

Darkness lit up, and demons scattered.
Guard the light, don't let me shatter.
I've been through some turbulence,
But with you, it all makes sense.

Let's never get off this orbit.
Everyone else seems so foreign.
Nothing connects like this.
Your gravity is reeling me in.

Sweet Temptation take me to forever.
Last ones on this earth together,
Fitting like puzzles pieces,
Blending into one flame eternally.

I HAD HOPED

I had hoped we would end up side by side.
And I had hoped you'd walk me down the aisle.
It was your life I wanted to complement mine.
I had hoped it would work out this time.

I had hoped all the love songs were about us.
And I had hoped you were the end of the search.
Every moment with you was another that made me sure.
I had hoped my eternal love was you.

And I don't know how I'm still alive, bearing this pain I feel.
Why did the doubts come along to wake me from my dream?

Now, my heart is broken, and I can't make things right.
You disappeared, and I don't know why.

I guess this is goodbye.

I had hoped we'd share our successes.
And I had hoped we'd grow old together.

It was a dream I wanted to realize.
I had hoped I'd always be with you.

REBECCA TORRELLAS

HALF OF MY HEART

I loved you unconditionally.
There's nothing that I wouldn't do.
So many adventures and plans.
What a world we made!

I barely had half of my heart left,
But you fixed what you could.
Then, when our future was inevitable
You took my heart and vanished.

Your ghost is haunting me.
I see you in everything.
It's so dark and lonely.
Half my heart is missing.

You were my savior
To help me from myself.
Where did you go?
I hate me. Who even am I?

You're gone, and I don't know why.
I don't feel like existing.
It's too hard to be in this place.
I'm so broken. Was I ever fixed?

    Why fight this? There's no point.
    This silence is so loud.
    The darkness is way too bright.
    I don't want to be here.

        I'll love you forever
        In the silent shadows
        Crying what's left of me.
        Barely enough to matter.

So, wherever you end up,
    Stay safe, stay happy
   So half of my heart
Can know what that is like.

REBECCA TORRELLAS

OFF-SCRIPT

We met while filming a movie.
I had a small part in a giant script.
You hated the way it was looking
And stole all the footage ever filmed...
Along with my heart.

We both wished on a shooting star
And that night, we both went off-script.
A one-night stand turned into moving in.
So many nights we'd sneak out of town...
To kiss all night.

The kisses scored by the rolling waves.
Remember your dad crashing our date?
The fireflies out in your family's land.
And the endless nights on the hammock...
"My passion is you."

We later made a movie together.
The chemistry jumped off the screen.
Every kiss filled with undying love

REBECCA TORRELLAS

You never wanted it to end...
No matter what.

But you weren't Gary Oldman
And I no Alanis Morissette.
Our intentions were clear,
But our execution faltered...
And you ran away.

After two and a half years, you disappeared.
Didn't even leave a break-up note.
I waited on the hammock for your return.
All alone with all this love...
With nowhere to go.

>I finished the last film I promised.
>I faked smiles as I finished it all.
>I waved goodbye to my colleagues.
>And heard the last note on the score...
>The credits rolled.

>And while the credits are rolling
>I still have all my invisible scars
>Reminding me of the adventures
>The passion and love that ended...
>Only for you.

I still find things at my house
That used to belong to you.
Pillows swelled with all my tears
The walls absorbed all my screams...
The hammock is gone.

With love having nowhere to go,
I started to type it all up.
A story about our romance
Keeping everything intact...
Except for how it ends.

Twelve books later, we're heroes.
Our story is finally told
About how we went off-script
And how the story continues...
The script's now mine.

Only mine.

Forever mine.

ARGUING WITH STARS

I try not to argue with stars
They're too beautiful to stay mad at.
I'd miss their sparkle and shine
Pulling me back again and again.

Your energy magnetized me.
Your brilliance captivated my soul.
Kissing under a falling star
We couldn't help but fall in love.

What a surprise, but horrible timing.
I had no idea what trauma was in me.
I couldn't figure out anything
Debilitated by fear of losing everything.

After I lost you, I looked at the stars
Telling them off one by one
Because they could still see you.
I even named one after you.

So, I stopped running, facing my demons
Accepting my past, figuring out the present.
No longer fearing who I'd become,
I moved forward wiser and stronger.

So here I am; I wish you could see me.
Finally attained the castle I dreamed of.
The stars finally aligned for me
Without a trace of you near me.

So maybe the stars knew what I didn't.
Maybe you don't deserve me at my best.
A star hasn't fallen since our first kiss.
Perhaps it was never meant to fall at all.

COULDN'T DO IT

I promised I'd wait forever,
But I couldn't do it.
Not because I didn't love you;
You couldn't love me through it.

The plan was to be together.
That's why I was waiting.
But I was abandoned;
Left in the bleachers hurting.

Not sure where you are now;
In love with me, yet disappeared.
So, I'm reluctantly moving on,
Living everything I feared.

REBECCA TORRELLAS

You said you'd always be here;
To wait for your return.
Then you punished me with silence,
Making my heart burn.

What a revelation;
The truth was always mine.
I guess you couldn't do it.
Don't worry, I'll be fine.

EXORCIZED

It's been over a decade since our hearts were intertwined.
Hiding off in our little world where you were never truly mine.

Passion swirled every night as we talked for hours.
For two and a half years, every star and planet was ours.

We talked about weddings, kids, and your dream of
being a grandfather.
The fireflies and shooting stars lit the way to our future together.

We cuddled up to documentaries and movies gracing the screen.
Intensely passionate outdoors with one eye open, daring being seen.

And I still remember the way you said you were in love with me
Cursing up at the sky, wishing the world could open an opportunity.

But I worked on it alone,
Not knowing I was already broken.
Too afraid to lose the one thing I wanted,
Leaving words unspoken.

And you became a ghost.
The love I wanted most.

For longer than it lasted,
Your disappearance was haunting me.
No closure, no break-up,
Just vanished so stunningly.

And maybe part of you always knew
You'd have to let me go
And you couldn't say it to my face because
you truly loved me so.

So I prayed a lot, trying to come to grips with how
It went, making self-amends.
It was no use. I kept seeing your face among the strangers
While out with friends.

I redecorated the house in an effort
To try to get you out of my memory,
Trying to erase the permanence
Of our intense love story.

I changed the keys; my pillow swelled with tears
As I tried to get through it alone.
Eventually, I found the pieces of my heart
And glued them on my own.

My greatest loss eventually became
the path to finding me and all I wanted.
I looked around at what my life had become —
I was no longer haunted.

I exorcised your ghost.
The one who hurt me most.

REBECCA TORRELLAS

CHANGED THE PROPHECY

You loved me like
I was your destiny.
The prophecy set
Just for you and me.

Beneath stars, UFOs, and fireflies
We made the universe ours
Chemistry exploding
Watching our worlds collide.

You didn't want to do
What you ultimately had to.
Calling me whatever you wanted
To make you feel better.

You don't know me. You never did.
I'm faithful, happy, prospering, blessed.
You're the one stuck in the small town
You were trying to get away from.

REBECCA TORRELLAS

You wanted me to be a cheater,
Stupid, crazy, and unstable
Just so you wouldn't have to disappoint
Those already at your table.

    He's faithful to me, too.
    No third girls, wives, or roommates.
    Hiding the things you refused to give up
    While wanting to be a grandfather someday.

        We could've had it all
        We could've had everything...
        But you left without a word
        So I went on my own instead.

For a time, you were all to me.
You left me for those you wouldn't leave
Even though you wanted to see it all burn
Then I was left to miss you.

    And miss you, I did.
    For what seemed an eternity.
    But as you kept your past intact
    My future opened up.

REBECCA TORRELLAS

        Now I got all I wanted
        While your dream of
        Being a grandfather crumbled
        Away with your decisions.

For a man who wanted truth
You lied to everyone you knew
Including to yourself.
I grew happy being out of that wolfpack.

        Not sure if you're happy
        Maybe you're full of regrets
        That I changed the prophecy
        And found a world of happy.

                And the funny twist
                To all the fates that were ours
                I'm the one of the two of us
                Not living lies anymore.

THE SO-CALLED TRUTH

Never on the lease, but I remember
How you always wanted truths,
But the one truth that mattered
Was you were never truly mine.

You asked for truths, but all they
Became were excuses to convince
Yourself to stay with the one
Who loves you, pretending I never did.

But I loved you. Deny it if it heals you
Of all the hell you put me through
Just to leave me there
Worse than you found me.

I would've died for you, yet you killed me.
Parts of me too gone to fix.
I mourned me, a broken spirit,
Inhabiting a ghosted island.

In time, my life changed for the better.
Without you, I was filled with grace.
A miracle granted from prayers unanswered.
Happiness I never imagined would come.

Yet all these years later, you're the same.
With the girl you cheat on, denying her wish.
She loves you; guess your lies are enough.
You knew they wouldn't work for me.

I got what she wanted out of life.
The one thing you wouldn't give her.
I'm the lucky one you gave away
Who lives in more truth than you ever have.

I look at life now, and I'm not bitter.
My worst days are still good.
I hope you're happy in the same place
You tried your hardest to escape from.

THE EXCHANGE

Close to a decade
And here I am sitting,
Holding the most beautiful thing
My eyes have ever witnessed.

> When you left, I thought
> I was going to die
> But I'm glad I held on
> Or I would've missed this.

God knew he was coming,
And it couldn't happen with you.
You claimed that you wanted this too.
That turned out not to be true.

> Now looking back as words
> Go in and out of my head,
> Like dreams and nightmares
> At night, while in bed.

Our masterpiece love connection
Secret languages and rendezvous
The promises sounded so solid
But your sin is now my adventure.

                    And when I look in his eyes
                    I know I lost you in exchange.
                    God's choice; I understand it now.
                    Cause I love him massively.

Just look at who I'm holding.
I'm a mother; he's my universe.
He repaired the half of my heart
You shattered to pieces.

                    I told you I'd love you forever.
                    I didn't lie; I wonder sometimes.
                    But the moment he laughs, I know
                    My life is perfect; more than enough.

It was agony to give you up,
But I made it through.
Strong enough to deserve him;
The exchange turned out perfectly.

I HOPE YOU'RE HAPPY

It took so long to finally come to terms
With the reality that you and I
Weren't meant to be a lifelong thing.

Even with a broken rearview mirror
I still catch glimpses in 20-20
That make me grateful for the outcome.

You knew that I wanted a family.
You knew you'd never quit certain things.
A bullet in the heart; a noble sacrifice.

The heart mended, and I'm finally fine.
My boy's eyes heal me all the time.
He came to me when my heart let you go.

Saw you recently; you still seem the same.
After all these years, you still spark the room.
It's refreshing; some things never change.

REBECCA TORRELLAS

I'm successful, can you believe it?
I'm a mother with a man who loves me.
I hope you're happy ... happy like me.

REBECCA TORRELLAS

If We Saw Each Other Now

If we saw each other now,
I'd have so much to say.
I'd have to stifle so much
Just to not take up your day.

    I'd like to tell you honestly
    Your absence almost killed me.
    That I waited and waited
    Crying to sleep almost nightly.

        I'd want to tell you I tried my best.
        I loved you more than I care to admit.
        I did way more than I should have done
        Not to lose you as I did.

        But what good would that do now?
        It's useless to apologize.
        I'm sure you had your reasons
        Regardless of my useless cries.

REBECCA TORRELLAS

I wrote so many emails
They're all still in my drafts.
Begging for answers while
Knowing too well all the facts.

    As time passed, so much changed.
    Miracles happened, I don't know how.
    It's funny to wonder what could've been
    But I'd miss what I have now.

        I hope you don't hate me
        Since I don't know what made it end.
        I'd be willing to start over
        And shake hands as a friend.

            I'd show you pictures
            Look at all this I've made.
            I'm so happy in this place.
            Look at the part you played.

    But I doubt you'd ever speak.
    It's just something I dream about.
    Not to relight, just closure
With someone I once couldn't live without.

REBECCA TORRELLAS

WITCH HUNT

REBECCA TORRELLAS

Weapons of Silence

I'm still trying to heal
All the burns in my mind.
So many silent shotgun
Shells still left to find.

Weapons of silence
Destroy a person's soul.
Years of friendship gone
Was that always the goal?

I'll never know what
Made you want me dead.
Act like you never even
Knew me as a friend.

I get that time moves on
And things are meant to change.
I thought we'd see each other
Laughing as we age.

REBECCA TORRELLAS

Was I not worth talking to?
Did I not act like an adult?
Or did I do something,
Just tell me it's my fault.

There's no closure when
No one says a word.
What did I do to make you
Trip me onto your sword?

Guess if I'm dead to you
You'll never see these words.
This is to heal me.
It can't get any worse.

I give up trying.
Consider me inexistent.
I hope I can do the same
Delete you in an instant.

HATEFUL BUTTERFLY

Butterfly, butterfly
Stuck in your hate;
Butterfly, butterfly
The smoke you create.

So lost in the roses are
The fingers you point.
Ignorant butterfly
Missing the fingerprint.

The thorns never wanted
To scratch any wolves.
Your jealousy and hate
Your lies make moves.

Only in your head
Do your enemies dance.
Butterfly, butterfly
You missed your chance.

You blame the roses
To veer all eyes
Butterfly, don't you know,
They see through your lies?

Your wings don't shine
Through buried rose petals.
Did you know, sweet butterfly,
They wear protective metals?

The thorns won the war.
They carried their cross.
While the hateful butterfly
Ignores her loss.

And it's sad, for you see
The roses are on fire.
Stronger than ever
They've never bloomed brighter.

Poor, sweet butterfly,
Carrying your lies.
Close to the ground
You defend your goodbyes.

Tiny butterfly
Your heart on trial
As memories of the truth
Challenge your denial.

Keep searching and looking
To justify your hate,
While the roses are blooming
In their beautiful fate.

Butterfly, butterfly
The winds will turn.
Your lies and wings
Will eventually burn.

And when all has collapsed,
Destroyed by the shockwave,
Butterfly, through tears
You'll see roses on the grave.

WITCH HUNT

You called the witch hunt.
You said to be afraid.
Flying on broomsticks
The exact words you said.

Yet you're the one who seems
To curse the day we met.
Block me on social media
Then spy on me on the internet.

It was you who made
vinegar jars and told the sky
To break up a couple
And get the guy.

Yet I deserve all the judgment.
Point at me and yell, "Be afraid!
Don't you see it's her fault
All this evil has been made?"

"Burn her! Burn her!
Make her die!
She must be vanquished
If we're to survive!"

Well, I've lived despite your pleas
And hanging me on the tree.
I never summoned the elements
Or the power of three.

I came when you asked
And needed my help.
Your spite burned blessings
In the hand that you dealt.

God knew my heart
Through tears I cried.
And to my prayers
With a smile, He replied.

I got gifts you knew I wanted.
And it hurts you to see me blessed.
Everyone else is still my friend.
No fallout from the evil you professed.

The bell has been rung; the fight is over.
I'll grab my broom and fly to my corner.
Living happily the rest of my life
Away from my eternal scorner.

REBECCA TORRELLAS

BODIES YOU SCAR

Every once in a while
I see your clever name
And my heart bears armor
To prevent more pain.

      My trip on the high road
      Disguised as acceptance.
      The anger has stayed,
      Since you have no repentance.

            It's sad to see your pretty face
            When I know who you really are.
            What a triumph is your disguise
            Hiding the bodies you scar.

So, keep pushing your pain.
Play the victim so well.
I've long since found mercy
Since I broke out of your cell.

My mind still remembers
Though the heart has run far,
Too far to forgive
The cause of my scar.

                May you soar far away,
                Away from me and mine.
                I don't want them victims
                Of you dimming their shine.

For what it's worth,
The anger inspires.
Reminders are used
To fuel my fires.

        May you disappear
        In the distance, go far.
        So my loved ones won't be
        Bodies you scar.

REBECCA TORRELLAS

YOU CAN HAVE HER

Went to wish her happy birthday
Saw we were no longer friends.
She chose to take your side
And never make amends.

I don't plan to fight.
I'm not even going to bother.
Ever since you left my life
It's only gotten better.

She was there when I found out
God was giving me all I wanted.
Look at my life now,
Karma made sure I won it.

So, you can have her.
I won't even say goodbye.
She was always seeing red,
Bleeding my peaceful sky.

REBECCA TORRELLAS

She wanted slaves. I wanted friends.
Simple life with no regrets.
She'd scratch them all, fight the world,
While I'm not placing bets.

Have fun hating on everyone,
Including those you claim to love.
Point your fingers, thrive in hate
Judging like gods from above.

Remembering all you said
About each other now is hilarious.
Blame me. That's fine. I'm out.
It was so ridiculous.

I always knew how this would end.
You set the traps; I never fell.
I'll just write and add to my collection
Let it out, let it go, and never dwell.

CLOSURE

I'll never know why.
All I did was punish myself.
What was said or done
That made you disappear?

I wanted to die.
All I could do was cry.
Waiting on some sort of answer
To close the swirls in my mind.

I was tired of losing
And not knowing why.
I was ready to apologize
Instead was bullied from afar.

So, I had to get closure.
Leave survival mode.
Had to burn it to ashes
To make it make sense.

So I wrote and kept writing.
Prescriptions with every letter.
Thousands of healing words later,
I had a story to tell.

It was more about my feelings
Than it has ever been about you.
But I thank you just the same
For waking up this inspiration.

REBECCA TORRELLAS

REBECCA TORRELLAS

RESTORATION

SCRAPS

There you are, looking at me
So distracted you bit your napkin.
Your eyes glimmer as sparks fly
I barely notice we are talking.

I've been so broken for so long.
Why would you even want me?
Love stopped being beautiful to me.
I've pushed it away expeditiously.

Made me love them unconditionally
Then they mistreat me, and I dare fight.
Now, I'm the crazy one reacting.
At no point was I ever right.

Caged, forced, dumped, and spit on
Guns pointed at me, hated and vilified.
There's no point in loving me.
They felt their actions were justified.

There's only scraps of me now.
I'm not worth your time.
You need so much superglue
To fix this shattered heart of mine.

I don't understand; why are you here?
Don't you know you should be running?
You always get any girl you want.
What are you thinking?

Haters will all laugh at you.
"Let's see what she'll put him through."
Tearing at my tortured soul,
Hoping I'll make the joke come true.

You look happy holding on to scraps.
I guess you really want to be mine.
Let's take it slow; I'll give it a try.
You've given me hope; let's take our time.

THE WRECKAGE

When I met you, my ledger was bleeding.
The wreckage was still smoking.
Silence had exploded my dreams,
Left them in ashes in a heap.

I stayed there waiting for it to resuscitate,
Refusing to accept my life had burned.
Between stones thrown and my matches
It was no surprise it all crashed down.

My past smoldering became the show,
Canceled by those who said they loved me.
Years later, you passed by the mess I made,
and I let you rummage through all the evidence.

Without judgment, you grabbed my hand.
Told me to let it all die where it crashed.
There was no point in keeping my life on hold.
That life wasn't mine anymore.

Like a jewel, you proudly showed me off.
And blessings poured abound.
And it hasn't stopped since that day.
Can you believe this gift we've received?

Now, butterflies flutter by in happiness.
All the horror got swept away.
The girl trapped in a nightmare
Was mad to be saved, and you did.

RESTORATION

It feels good to want to be home.
It feels crazy to have a family of my own.
It came together like magic.
A miracle I'd never experienced before.

So many times, I tried to make it work.
Maybe it wasn't worth all the hurt.
But what an unbelievable twist of fate.
I didn't have to be alone anymore.

Friends healing hearts turned into lovers.
And before long, some unexpected wonders.
This little baby came for us to raise him
How could this even happen to me?

Cause I was always the invisible one
That most threw out and left behind.
The forgettable, not worth the trouble
Left crying where no one would see.

Thrown under buses for protection.
"She'll forgive us without objection."
Gaslit to make me think I was crazy.
Tearing everything about me apart.

But you resurrected my loving spirit.
So blessed, I cannot believe it.
I can't get enough of this journey.
Thank you for restoring my heart.

COFFEE VIBES

Coming home to you;
Our own piece of paradise.
It's not postcard blue
But it hits me just fine.

                    Can relax and be myself;
                    I'm not under scrutiny.
                    Be a mom and release
                    All my supported creativity.

Enjoying all these colors;
Shades of bright are new to me.
You don't have a clipboard
Judging all my history.

                    Our son is a daily gift.
                    A surprise heaven sent.
                    Easy to see miracles
                    In all the time we've spent.

It's funny how quickly
It all came together
When we finally gave
A chance to forever.

                    Vibes like a cup of coffee
                        Hug my heart so right
                 Comfort and peace and love
               Gets me through every night.

          And no matter what colors
              We may be seeing.
           There is no other place
            I'd rather be in.

SHOWING UP

Thank you for being
The man of the house.
For actually showing up.

No matter what is needed
You figure it out in plenty.
Thank you for showing up.

Do you know how many men
Walk away or ghost or leave
A family off to their own defenses?

And to think you never wanted one
And then you reached for me
And suddenly, we're a family.

Even in our darkest days
I know we're safe because you're here
Bravely showing up.

Our happiness clearly on his face.
Our little boy just laughing away.
That's the reward for showing up.

As a friend, I'm proud of you
As your lover, I love you.
I'm blessed because you kept showing up.

You changed everything
And you brought me peace
Just by showing up.

And we love you a million times.
An answered prayer
You showing up.

READY TO BE HOME

Today has been particularly hard.
It's been raining all over my heart.
One of those days colored in grays.
It's worse when we have to be apart.

I've been working hard every day.
Just feels like it's not going my way.
Ready to be home. Don't want to be alone.
Can I pick you two up and just run away?

Things are fine, yet I'm coming undone.
Hiding my pain from everyone.
I'm not on my game. It just stays the same.
There is no chance this fight can be won.

Coming home just fixes it all.
Hugs and laughter, having a ball.
Now I'm at peace. The world can cease.
Our own little planet where I never fall.

AT LAST

It's nice to feel at peace
Every time we're all at home.
To see the three of us smile,
No matter where we roam.

I always wanted a family.
It took so long to find it.
Then miracles came so fast,
And the pieces finally fit.

When you first found me,
All I was focused on was my past.
You don't care I didn't love you first.
You do everything so we will last.

It's not always easy,
But it's never been that hard.
It's healing to be in this place.
My heart feels so unscarred.

And all the naysayers
Have been proven wrong.
We've surprised them all
We ended up being this strong.

I'm so happy we're here.
With our friends all together.
How did we get this lucky?
Blessed in so much love forever.

I've forgiven and forgotten
Even those who never asked.
And all the mistakes I made
God forgave me at last.

This is all proof of that.

REBECCA TORRELLAS

I REMEMBER IT ALL

HEADLINE

Nightmares on paper and ink
Trying to make you think
It's entertaining.

                        Kids with guns at school
                     Another drunk driving fool.
                        Criminals are killing.

      A few dollars get you into another's misery.

Another house catches fire
Someone else blows a tire
Glad it's not me.

                        Armed robbery is reported
                        Politics are distorted
                        How can this be?

           Maybe someday it will be me.

There's more than just one source.
Pain caused with no remorse.
Victims were just in the way.

> You can't help but read about it.
> What's the headline today?
> What does the headline say?

Get to know the world.

Another racist remark.
There's a rape at the park.
They're so heartless.

> Killing people for land.
> Peace they don't understand.
> They couldn't care less.

Now they're famous on the top story.

Another airplane goes down.
An earthquake rocks a town.
It's all so tragic.

Houses lost in a flood.
                        A child is covered in blood.
                        Mother in a panic.

While the good news is buried.

    What's the headline today?
    What does the headline say?
      Will it be me someday?

      Isn't it all entertaining?

Holding On To Nothing

Remembering all the times we spent.
The sweetest times God ever sent.
It's amazing what memories can do.

Now I feel I'm going out of my mind.
We'd been best friends for the longest time.
How do I make it back to you?

I loved you for so long
And I don't know what went wrong.
Are you waiting in line for a new thing?

How can love fade so fast?
I thought that this would last.
When was I holding on to nothing?

I don't want anyone new.
I've been so used to being with you.
How can this be the end?

You worked so hard to get me by your side.
Didn't think that'd be the end of the ride.
Now, you're barely my friend.

Being with you was perfection.
It stings to know it was deception,
And I was holding on to nothing.

DISRESPECTED

All you had to do was call me out.
But no... you had to make it personal.
I make mistakes. I own up.
Now, I have to bring my arsenal.

What the hell is wrong with you?
Trust is hard to mend.
Here's a giant middle finger
I should've never called you friend.

You threw a hissy fit
And now you're fine.
All full of smiles
While the stress is all mine.

The tire marks from the bus
Stain the road with my blood
From the knives on my back
And the tears cause a flood.

I prayed for your health.
That has since ended.
You won't apologize ever
So, we will never be mended.

I now pray you move away.
Maybe to France, Australia, or Spain.
Where the sound of your name
Can stop causing any more pain.

After this poem
My voice will silence.
My emotions I will hide
To survive this forced alliance.

Disrespected, this heart of mine
Forever will stay.
God, please answer my prayer
And make her go away.

From me... forever... away...

I Remember It All

I remember his touch, so soft and passionate.
He made you feel like you could do it all.
The kind who listens and understands
When your world seems to fall.

I remember it all, brand new to me.
We fit together in a perfect set.
I wish he could remember all the things
I'm trying my hardest to forget.

I think, "He's the one to lose it all!"
In me, he had his biggest fan.
But it's hard to believe that when you know
For me, he was the perfect man.

He knew what to say; he knew what to do.
Now, my heart is one big mess.
Even though he's left and hurt me
I don't love him any less.

REBECCA TORRELLAS

I hope one day he remembers
What once seemed pure and perfect.
And remembers the beautiful things
I soon hope to forget.

Will It?

For years, shackles adorned his feet.
They're saying dead man walking.
The seconds slowly creep away
As he's silently praying:

    Will I ever get to heaven this way?

        He lies down and sees
      The family of the man he murdered.
       Remembering the crime scene
        Under his breath, he mutters:

Will I ever see God's face someday?

As the poison enters
He sees his own family
Who still loves him dearly.
Suddenly, he lay peacefully.

I'm sorry, I hope I see you in heaven this way.

STUPID ONE

Your dreams have all come true
As she's walking down the aisle.
Your heart will beat with her every breath
For the rest of your life.

Between the candles and the roses
I sit in the back
All alone in a long black dress
Mourning the past.

As the music begins to play
I keep thinking back to that day
When fear overcame love, and I said no.
I'm the stupid one who let you go.

And as you make your solemn vow
My mind travels back in time
To the day when you wanted me
So many years ago.

When I was so in love with you
And you confessed your desires to me.
I was so scared you'd shatter my heart
I made you walk away.

We will never know what might have been.
Would things still be the same?
If my heart hadn't been so afraid of you
Would that be me bearing your name?

She's officially your wife.
As you move in for the kiss
There's a glow that fills the room
From the smile on your face.

I wipe the tears from my eyes
And tell my heart to say goodbye.
I wish you well, my love.
This is meant to be.

STAGE FRIGHT

A different actress takes the role
After the last one didn't work out.
You get the lines and moves just right.
But on opening night, you can't be found.

So there stands your bride, all dressed in white.
She won't be throwing her bouquet tonight.
You ran away with stage fright again.
Dreams are shattered as you drive away.

The shiny diamond turns a shade of blue
As she takes it off to give back to you.
She blames herself for you walking away,
And you let her leave in shame.

What is it that scares you away?
Is it the lights or the "forever" line?
The tux is rented, and so are you.
Love's not enough to get you through.

Maybe one day you'll find
The love that fits just right
Before you buy ring number three
Work through your stage fright.

CHANGE YOUR MIND

They don't care what you have to say.
They want you to do it their way.
Is it them, or is it you?

You want to find out on your own,
But they'd rather you be safe at home.
Don't let them tell you what to do.

Follow your heart,
Don't let them change your mind.
Do what you want now;
This is your time.

Fight for yourself.
This is your life.
No matter what they say,
Don't let them change your mind.

You know what you want to do,
But they have other plans for you.
They don't like what you've been dreaming.

Don't be afraid to fight.
Stand your ground and hold on tight.
You have something to believe in.

Follow your heart,
Don't let them change your mind.
It's up to you
To make things right

For yourself,
See what you find.
Don't let them say
You have to change your mind.

REBECCA TORRELLAS

REBECCA TORRELLAS

END OF THE TUNNEL

Winning Streak

Are you mad
That I said what I said?
Did you expect it
To die in my head?

You're the one
Who created this "me."
Inspired all the
Timeless creativity.

You lured me to you;
Convinced me to love you
So unconditionally that I
Forgot to love me, too.

You all became a team
Superheroes against me.
Made me a villain,
Screamed so convincingly.

You kicked me out
And threw your thorns.
I cried alone
As you blew your horns.

Thought I'd be canceled
With all the hate I faced.
To my surprise,
I was embraced.

Thanks to you
I'm stronger than ever.
Your words of hate
Just made me stronger.

You stayed in your circles
Talking about those you despise
I cried for so long
Before I came to realize.

I was out of that place,
The toxic had kicked me out.
What had seemed so unfair
Was sending me another route.

I stayed at home alone
I quietly let it unfold.
I let karma reveal
The stories left untold.

I thought I was going to die.
I needed to save my heart.
Then inspiration took a strike;
Showed me where to start.

Tears of blood became ink;
The freedom gave me a voice.
Once I started, it was like
A master who gave me no choice.

It spilled out of me
From a stream to a waterfall.
There were stories to tell once
I wasn't locked down at all.

And it's all because of you;
Look at who I've become.
I now have a voice
And a beat to my own drum.

So The Evil, the witch,
The whore, the liar, the freak
Turned it all around
Into a winning streak.

Does it make you upset
That you're the reason
I fought my way
Into a winning season?

Even my bad days
Are beautiful ones.
There's only a few losses
In the good runs.

Look at my family and friends
The ones you grew to hate.
We're constantly celebrating
Our collected fate.

We're all so happy.
Our bonds are strong.
Did it happen because
You didn't come along?

In all this wonder,
Thank you for the mess
That brought me to this place
Of peace and happiness.

Without you,
Where would I be?
Likely not where I am
So incredibly happy.

So, if you're mad,
You made this monster.
Knock me down again
I'll just get up faster.

If you want to hate,
Point at me and start poaching.
Remember who it was
I looked to for coaching.

Thank you again
For all the hate you speak.
You're the reason for the season;
My endless winning streak.

REBECCA TORRELLAS

THE END OF THE TUNNEL

The light at the end of the tunnel of pain
Will always be a wiser, stronger version of you.
The longer you stay in the tunnel,
Allowing someone to take advantage of you,
The longer it will take you to get to the light
Because the person enslaving you
Doesn't want you to see the light.
No matter how dependent you feel on them for love
Or how happy you think they make you,
They will always drag you down.
They won't follow you into the light.
It's safer for them to keep you in the dark.
Don't accept it. Free yourself.
Eventually, the light heals you.
The right lover... the right friends...
Won't drag you into a tunnel and leave you there.
You are special. You are cherished. You are bright.
Now, go out there and shine like the light you are.

Want more? There are more books to check out at
rebeccat.com

If you enjoyed this collection of poetry, please leave
a review. Thank you so much for reading!

Visit rebeccat.com to see other books by Rebecca Torrellas.

REBECCA TORRELLAS

Check out the **Howl Series**, *an urban fantasy four-book series by*
Rebecca Torrellas

Sierra, a human orphan adopted by the Rose Moon pack, grows up alongside her best friend, Xayden, the pack's future Alpha. As they navigate through the changes his 18th birthday brings, an unexpected twist of fate has them running for their lives. With targets on their backs, they partner with their friends to find those responsible for the attacks — both physical and mystical. But will their investigation get too close for those with secrets to hide? How much is a life worth when the future of the pack is at stake?

HOWL at the WATER
HOWL at the WIND
HOWL at the FIRE
HOWL at the EARTH

Join the Mailing List

Visit Official Website

For more information, visit howlseries.com.

Look for the upcoming urban fantasy
warrior fairy book series:

WINGS & THORNS

Created by Rebecca Torrellas

She never imagined one glance would have such disastrous consequences. When a tiny fairy encounters a breathtaking human, her heart thumps, and her wings flutter. She should have flown away, but the forbidden allure was too irresistible.

When the human is kidnapped under mysterious circumstances, she and her best friend risk everything to save his life. As they dig deeper into the enigma, nothing is as it seems. Sinister forces have diabolical plans, and the duo must convince the other fairies in their colony to help rescue the human — a sworn enemy. But a bigger threat is on the horizon. Their actions come at a grave cost, and the colony may not be strong enough to face a powerful foe.

Alliances will be forged. Sacrifices made. But will it be enough? The fate of the humans and the fairies is at stake.

Join the Mailing List   Visit Official Website

For a list of all published and upcoming books in this series, visit the official website:
www.wingsandthorns.com

AUDIOBOOKS

The audiobook for "Thorns In The Rose" is now available. For more information click on the QR code.

Narrated by Cesalina Davidson, Laura Coccimiglio, Amira Judeh, Sarah-Beth Diller, Christie Guidry, Bailey Hampton, and Rachel Brownhill.

About The Author

Rebecca Torrellas is the writer and creator of the four-part saga called the "Howl Series," featuring books "Howl at the Water," "Howl at the Wind," "Howl at the Fire," and "Howl at the Earth." The series tackles themes including unrequited love, loyalty, responsibility, family dynamics, and the bonds of friendship.

In December 2018, she also released a standalone romantic comedy titled "One Time at the River," a hilarious story about star-crossed lovers at the river.

She's currently working on "Wings & Thorns," an ongoing urban fantasy series about love, friendship, loyalty, betrayal, and abuse of power among fairies that escalates into the human world, jeopardizing both humans and each other.

Torrellas has also begun a production company, RoseFae Entertainment, producing book trailers and audiobooks in partnership with Marcus Sabom and his company, Friend Indeed Productions. The audiobooks to "Wings & Thorns" have a full cast featuring over 100 actors.

Torrellas earned a Bachelor of Arts degree in journalism at Texas A&M University. She worked at several newspapers throughout the state, including the Bryan-College Station *Eagle* and the Brenham *Banner-Press*.

She moved to Houston, where she worked as an editor, consumer reporter, and designer for a non-profit newsletter. She later became a managing editor and web editor for an international trade magazine in the oil and gas industry. She is currently the managing editor for an award-winning trade publication in Houston, Texas.

Always the creative, Torrellas has released two alternative rock albums, "No Hard Feelings" and "Let the Drama Begin," and also acted in several films, including the upcoming "The Good Friend," written and directed by Sabom. She also runs a sports broadcasting website, Legacy Sports Network (lsnsports.com), and edits a book series by fellow author

Tripp Ellis.

She finds inspiration for her stories in her daily experiences with friends, family, and those she's loved, lost, and admired. When not working, she finds joy in spending time with the loves of her life, Brian, and their son, Braxton.

www.ingramcontent.com/pod-product-compliance
Lightning Source LLC
LaVergne TN
LVHW091256080426
835510LV00007B/279